Thin Ice

Elisabeth Rowe

Oversteps Books

First published in 2010 by   Oversteps Books Ltd
                                 6 Halwell House
                                 South Pool
                                 Nr Kingsbridge
                                 Devon
                                 TQ7 2RX
                                 UK

www.overstepsbooks.com

Copyright © 2010 Elisabeth Rowe
ISBN 978-1-906856-15-1

All rights reserved. No part of this book may be reproduced, stored in a retrieval system, or transmitted in any form, or by any means, electronic, mechanical, photocopying, recording or otherwise, or translated into any language, without prior written permission from Oversteps Books, except by a reviewer who may quote brief passages in a review.

The right of Elisabeth Rowe to be identified as the author of this work has been asserted by her in accordance with the Copyright, Designs and Patents Act 1988.

Printed in Great Britain by imprint digital, Devon.

Supported by the
National Lottery through
the Arts Council England

*For Anthony Rowe
and Roselle Angwin*

Mindful of words

Exquisite!
With our love
Rodney & Patrick
Sept 2010

Acknowledgements:

Some of these poems have appeared in The Interpreter's House, Artemis, Private international review of photographs and Private online.

Competition prizes were awarded for the following poems:
2nd prize; Going to School (Peterloo Poets), Big Girl (Virginia Warbey), Amaryllis (Wells)
5th prize: The General (Peterloo Poets) and Wilderness Looms (Poetry on the Lake)

Other poems that have been short-listed or commended:
Blue (Second Light), Wanting to be Real (Split the Lark), Love Letters (Ware Poets), Mind Lodes and Casting Off (Kent and Sussex), Several Kinds of Ordinary Happiness (Ilkley), Koikkala Summer Market (Words by the Water), Gethsemane (Strokestown), Human Writes (Wells) and The Undertaker's Lament (Poetry on the Lake).

Contents

Disillusion	1
Going to School	2
Admonition	3
Blue	4
The Plan	5
Un-permitted	6
Big Girl	7
An Introduction To Child Pruning	8
Cowboy Summer	9
Wanting to Be Real	10
Love Letters	11
Archaeologist	12
Dusk	13
Your Silences	14
The Edge	15
Mind Lodes	16
Casting Off	17
Several kinds of ordinary happiness	18
Portrait	19
Afterwords	20
Englishwoman in Tuscany	21
Ice Queen In The Sauna	22
Amaryllis	23
Koikkala Summer Market	24
Bird-watching	25
Äkäsmylly	26
Shadows	28
Wilderness Looms	30
The Clearances	31
Otherwise	33
Gethsemane	34
Irreconcilables	35
The General	36
Ivy	37
Home Visit to the Sea	38
The Undertaker's Lament	39

Shimla	40
Another Day	41
There Be Dragons	42
Shadow Selves	43
The Rope Bridge	44
Bequest	45
Larks	46
Thin Ice	47
Sorry	48
Human Writes ...	50

Disillusion

He was coming home from the war,
my mother said.

I'd never seen my father
but I saw the two of us running,
my father catching me, swinging me
high in the air.

He would call me Elisabeth
and I wouldn't mind.

I started walking.
The lane spilled fizzy white flowers,
and lazy planes droned overhead
like little bees.

I know now that we are all looking for a father.

It was the post man who found me,
hoisted me on the cross-bar of his bicycle,
and pedalled me home.

I found a strange man in the front room,
hugging my mother and laughing;
he held out his hand
but I ran away,

went back down the lane
to look for my father who was coming
home from the war.

Going to School

It was a safe, every day event: flinging
my bicycle at the station railings,
two-at-a-timing to the far platform
as the train snuffled under the footbridge
sneezing white speech balloons,
to subside in an agony of steel
and a long hissing sigh of relief.

In the empty nicotine-thick compartment
I'd wrestle the leather window strap,
lean out to pepper my plaits with smuts;
treading the greasy brown moquette
I'd swing from the luggage nets,
rub shoulders with pale alien prints
of Lyme Regis and Budleigh Salterton.

And so the world went by to the soft
iambic clacking of wheels on tracks,
the funnelled grunt and strain of steam:
all those innocent green fields
giving way to shoebox gardens,
the gas works and the railway works,
the one-eyed porter on Ashford station

until the day I watched a man lean out
to wave from the carriage window; saw
a woman freeze-framed on the platform
reach across the distance between them;
glimpsed the man's face as the tunnel grabbed
his arm and broke it, and knew suddenly
that the world would never be a safe place.

Admonition

'Don't sit on the wet grass,' she says,
'or you'll get piles.' But what are piles?
Like pensions, they belong in some
alternative universe, and anyway
the grass is cool and sweet.

Wise children learn early to scorn
such admonitions, trusting in
the five-times Now! of their senses,
unencumbered by the fear
of surly consequence.

Too soon they must inherit a world
brimming with treachery: rip tides,
bogs and precipices beckon,
deviants and maniacs flourish,
gravity springs its trap.

I advise sitting on damp grass
as often as possible, not waiting
till age makes a foolish pleasure
of transgression, but spawning
a whole dynasty of piles.

Blue

She brings him the egg still warm in the nest of her hands,
a perfect freckled blue like the eye of heaven.

Holding it gently between gnarled finger and thumb
he pierces it with a needle, north and south,
makes a soft egg-shape with his lips and blows:

the filmy dribbles of silver, the threads of gold
quicken a fledgling hurt she cannot name.

One day in her perfect blue emptiness she will remember
the crushed shell in her hands like pieces of sky
flecked with blood, the assiduous thrush still singing.

The Plan

When you are tempted to be a child again,
stamp your foot and cry, 'Look at me! Look at me!'
or press a threadbare comfort blanket to
your cheek, to fold out the loneliness;

when you need to see the world re-made
in primary colours neatly edged with black
and yourself painted round like a sun with rays
of arms and legs and a mouthful of futures:

remember how it felt to be marooned
among the spoiled fragments of delight,
laughing because you couldn't say it hurt;

how in the darkness all the little harms
came flocking, whispering that grief
like disappointment was part of the plan.

Un-permitted

There is a kind of rage that is
born of concealment, a skill
learned early like darning, patching
and dipping a knife in boiling water
to smooth the sharp white icing;

a habit as nice and necessary
as holding open the door and
giving your seat to the elderly;
never losing your temper
or speaking ill of the living.

You bury the bad feelings,
resentments, mortifications and
forbidden thoughts – conceal them
like so many tons of rubbish
dumped in a landfill site,

not knowing the destiny
of all such un-permitted things,
how they compress beneath the sweet
green surface, brewing a mephitic
heat that craves release.

You never foresee the shock:
rage, seeking a fracture in the crust,
a rift in the landscape of composure,
discharges with the disproportionate
violence of surprise.

Big Girl

Dinner dance at the Ritz.
The cousins are down from Scotland:
slender pony-faced girls with tartan sashes,
overgrown boys thrilling in kilts
and rugby knees.

She's up from the Kentish countryside:
champion tree-climber, bicyclist, spy.
Her breasts are bound in merciless
bright blue chiffon,
her net petticoats jut like a ballerina's
but she cannot dance.
Her hands and feet no longer belong to her,
her smile is petrified.
At school she always had to be the man:
sometimes they partnered chairs.

The aunts encourage her with loud halloos,
the uncles slide by,
averting their gaze benignly.
Only her brother grips her wrists
and steers her anti-clockwise round the
thrumming floor.

Oh the impenetrable agony
of Scottish reels!
She will never quite get over this:
big girl at the dance, sleep-walking,
knowing she may have to wait a hundred years
for the one who will see into her heart
and kiss her awake.

An Introduction To Child Pruning

Pruning children is recommended if you want to
Stimulate growth. Here are some of the basic
Principles to observe:

The purpose of pruning is to achieve either
Maximal ornamental effect (see chapter on girls)
Or optimum yield (ditto boys).

Consider the rootstock, for this will determine
The child's vigour. The poorer the conditions
The lighter the pruning should be.

Although some children flourish despite neglect,
Most are known to respond to a regular
Programme of management.

Carry out remedial pruning of stunted behaviour,
Excising dead, diseased and damaged growth.
(N.B. Some long whippy kids

Will straighten out and stiffen if left to themselves).
A child with a naturally upright habit should not
Be forced horizontally.

When dealing with ramblers and climbers, timely
Formative pruning and training will establish
Well-furnished personalities.

Train climbers when development is young and pliant.
Cut back leaders to vigorous shoots, not forgetting
To remove suckers.

Contrary to expectation, you should adopt
A lighter touch with vigorous growth, tackling
Weak formation fiercely.

A word of warning: some children may bleed
If wounded, and become vulnerable to damage
By frost and wind.

Finally, ensure that those to whom you entrust
The care of your children are provided with suitable
Well-sharpened tools.

Cowboy Summer

Fifty years since I rode out with a ranch boy
under the great blue hammock of sky
slung between Rocky Mountain peaks
and prairie thermals.

It was the New World, I was in the foothills,
sloughing my old world village innocence,
the grammar school, the trudging post-war years,
belief in progress, whatsoever things etc.

I rode that summer western style,
peg-legged in the saddle, feet wedged
into wooden stirrups, reins held proud.
Once, when we had dismounted and lay
flattening bristled Indian paint-brush,
ox-eye daisies and coarse grasses,

I told him I was not that kind of girl,
and he rolled off and lit a cigarette;
the horses grazed nearby, snorting pollen
while we stared up at the galloping white clouds,
their streaming manes and tails.

That was the summer the Cisco kid
rode the stampede parade. He waved to me,
but I already knew I'd never learn
the fierce unbridled confidence
I longed for, self-belief as boundless
as those tracts of heaven and earth:

the old world was calling me home
to ride the sharp green future English style,
all balance, nothing to grip or brace myself against,
the sky a small inverted bowl of dreams.

Wanting to Be Real

I want to be real. I'm sick of waiting in the
empty restaurant, white napkin over my arm:
tables are laid, candles lit, yet nobody comes.

I confess I have no taste for extremity,
wouldn't relish starvation, hugging stones,
swallowing substances or crossing continents

to sit swathed in saffron at the feet of seers:
but I want a life that's more than the sum of its parts,
I want to believe in things. People who know

are real: I watch their smiles leave bite marks;
my knowing is insubstantial as sea-water
poured by a child into a hole in the sand.

I might fail to recognise my own reality
if it burrowed my skin to travel my blood-ways;
if it came like a lover or perhaps a torturer

snapping finger bones. I need something obvious,
like walking through the door marked 'Arrivals'
to find someone holding a placard with my name.

I came close to it once: watched my face in the glass
beginning to move, but it was the other train
that was moving and somebody else's face.

Love Letters

They smell of things that have been kept too long.
I know the writing, and the blue black ink
from your Parker fountain pen, that old address.
It was Larkin time, everything just after

or just before. I scan the heady rhetoric
that flares across the page like tracer fire,
feel nothing but the sadness and the shame
of not remembering that I was beautiful

and loved. I'll leave them for someone else
to find, as I found my father's wartime letters
to my mother, discovering in those frail
grey pages and tiny censored scrawl

two intimate strangers, knowing myself
for the first time an extra in their script.

Archaeologist

Not satisfied with surfaces
I'll peel you back,
peg and quarter your topography
brushing away a lifetime's
soft protective silt.

I'll excavate the corbelled
enclave of your ribs,
expose the beating heart;
looking for coin hoard,
grave goods, hafted axe

and something more:
a whiff of wood-smoke,
sheep's wool, struggle,
blood. And if I find
nothing but hack-silver

among the hearth-waste
I'll not disguise my
disaffection: you'll be
a brief footnote in a
book of burial mounds.

Dusk

Light ebbs with the tide;
a serpent river uncoils
from the mud-flats.

I could reach out my hand
and part the thickening dusk
like hung muslin.

The last heron abandons
his station, ghostly pale.
My back grows cold.

You are all the thoughts
I may not touch, like cracks
in the pavement:

what if, avoiding love,
I fall in step with hate?
A round moon rises

over the hill, spilling
tintacks on the oiled
blackness of water;

and one by one lights
flare beyond the estuary
for other home-comings.

Your Silences

I never knew what to make of them:
imagined it was something
I had said or done.

You could say I was a connoisseur
of silences: acquainted
with power games,

playground punishments and prayer,
and the speechlessness
of tired couples.

But you quite simply absented yourself
as others left London
for the weekend

or disappeared into sheds or boats:
an act of sabotage
that itched me

to break those silences, to break out
of my own baffled hurt;
that hungered me

to be the one who tongued you into
cries of flame before
the last silence.

The Edge

We quarrelled all the way up
(something and nothing,
the wrong thing)

and when we reached the top
you stood knee-deep
in whitest mist,

stretching your arms to the sky,
lifting your face
to the sun;

and I saw how simply, how fiercely
you loved the world
and I hated you.

You were standing close to the edge.
As I reached out,
you turned, smiling,

you knew my intention even as it
flickered and died.
Afterwards

the knowledge lay between us
in the dark, the press
of our bodies

could not crush it. I went back
to the mountain, couldn't
even remember

why we quarrelled, only that
you were standing
close to the edge.

Mind Lodes

You going down, me following
according to custom: no warning
grumble of winding gear, just that
jolt as the cage begins to lurch
down the blind shaft. Water seeping
from the rock gleams like fool's silver;
old ghosts peer with blood-shot eyes
from shadowy adits.

We fear these mind lodes yet we still
stumble down that rough-hacked tunnel
beneath the granite seabed and the grey
Atlantic. The air is gunpowder-thick.
The ocean weighs heavily above us,
and some crazed acoustic serves
to funnel tinselly dance music from
liners far out to sea.

What kind of emotional economics
drives us to work these seams, far
from the salt sea breeze, the sunlight
snagging on blades of grass? We should
be mindful of the failed beam, the
failed pump, the crushed and drowned,
the women and children waiting up there
in Sunday black.

Casting Off

Just as any boat
could be nothing other than a boat –
  by the hollow
    the ribbed hull
      the bladed bow of it
fashioned for passage,

so each one of us
can serve only his known purposes –
  by the imperfect
    marriage of
      soul and sinew
furnished for singularity.

Still we believe
we can shape others to our own desires –
  by our tenderness
    our obduracy
      our sullen hunger
fasten them to our mooring;

or when that fails
fit ourselves to their curved hull and prow –
  for the casting off
    on the flood tide
      for the same old voyage
to the fortunate isles.

Several kinds of ordinary happiness

You are standing at the dressing table
making tea, one hand behind your back
like a fancy waiter.

The sea is so close we might be on a ship.
A gull lets go of the wind, slices the grey sky.
Boats tug at their leashes.

You tilt the mirror. I am still adrift
on the white pillows as you make a nest
of stones on the white quilt.

Whatever the life hereafter, there will be
both heaven and hell for most of us,
as there is here,

but now you come back to bed, taking care
not to disturb the nest, and we drink tea,
waiting for high tide.

Portrait

I watch them file past
murmuring as they shift position,
'How mysterious, the way the eyes
keep following us.'

But when I study your face
I find as your conservator an earlier
underlying sketch beneath the skin's
familiar craquelure,

where bone is fleshed out
and cynic lines about the eyes
smooth into the bold immortal
stare of youth.

It is not love that's blind,
only indifference, which sees nothing
beneath the brittle surface lacquer
honeyed with age.

No one else notices the mouth,
how it has softened with the years,
so I shall obscure this pentimento
in the heart's archive.

Afterwords

It's not just your body
that I shall mourn,
its worn invisible
cloak of closeness;
for all its sweetness
it was often absent,
suffered alteration,
a toll of treachery;

nor even your soul,
which went about
its own soul business
gleaning promises,
tracking abstractions,
while my divining
often discovered
nothing but iron;

but the missing self,
the one I created
solely for you,
the one you always
reflected cloudlessly,
which has no life
beyond this collusion
and no memorial.

Englishwoman in Tuscany

Alien as the rose
planted at the end
of each row of vines
to catch the sickness

She looks so cool
under her floral hat
sipping Brunello
di Montalcino

She is high on the
iconography
of agony, those
Tuscan crucifixions

She is in love with
every etiolated
marble Christ
in every pieta

Heat breaks in thick
honeyed waves
her body shudders
in the press of noon

The red wine spills
on the white cloth
blood and roses
her timid ecstasy

Ice Queen In The Sauna

She steps in
tall and firm as a birch,
not young but glassy
beautiful.

We have seen her
throned with the Ice King,
measured ourselves
against her glimmer.

We shuffle a space
with sullen fealty,
and hug our knees
uneasy in the rolling

landscape of our flesh.
When she throws water
onto hot stones
we do not flinch,

but leave to crush
snow onto our breasts
and stand burning
in the frozen air.

Amaryllis

Amaryllis slaps mosquitoes from
her bird-boned wrists,
her ninety seven years neatly filed
between wing-span shoulder pads
in eloquent polyester.

When she speaks
her eyes swim towards light.
She might have stepped straight from a
Schjerfbeck self-portrait (later period):
eyes asymmetrical, skin drum-tight
over the tiny skull.

'In nineteen sixteen' (someone translates)
'my father rode in the last charge
of the Russian cavalry. In those days
Finland belonged to Russia. Mind you,
we had to leave St. Petersburg in a hurry
during the Revolution.'

A hundred years, almost, of a life
meshed with violent history.
I am unequal to the task of crossing
so many frontiers, can only guess
which is more real to her:

a horseman galloping towards the guns,
a frightened girl fleeing a stricken city,
an old woman outliving another luminous
summer night in another century.

Koikkala Summer Market

This is the way of things in Koikkala:
a sleepy Saturday, some makeshift stalls
in a mown enclosure, no one in a hurry
to sell us thick-knit socks or berry pancakes.
Summer lets slip the ordinary burdens:
the elders turn their faces to the sun,
the women gossip peaceably, their children
chase one another in a cloud of seed-heads.

An old man leans on a trestle table heaped
with baskets woven in the ancient way
from strips of pine, with twisted birch-wood handles.
Someone has patterned bands of lichen grey
and fox-red bark among the honeyed pine.
Imagine coming from the forest in late summer
with baskets brimful of fluted chanterelles,
fat blueberries and blood-red lingonberries!

He fetches shoes crafted from ribbons of bark
peeled from the silver birch when sap is lively:
underneath lies a silky cinnamon lining
to cut and fold into origami footwear.
He probably wore shoes like this as a child,
like the young girl with accusing soot-rimmed eyes
in Jarnefelt's painting of exhausted wage-slaves
burning tree-stumps in the Finnish wilderness.

These small things are priceless, rooted deep
in time and place: through them we apprehend
the strong mysterious pulse of distant lives.
Next year there may not be a summer market
in Koikkala: even here things are changing.
Last week's golden dandelion fields
are all white-haired now, and the cuckoo
is already singing out of tune as we leave.

Bird-watching

Everything bears down from the north today:
high winds swan-feathering the cloud;
waves dashing headlong into the bay;
light leaping like a hare along the rocks.
When the lake stills, it almost brims over
the earth's curvature, holding the inverted sky
as a careful child might carry a bowl of milk.

Two swans ride the black and silver pathways
at the farther shore like a visitation from
some mythic world of pastoral innocence.
And all afternoon the blue tits come and go,
slipping deftly through an acid leaf-screen
to the nesting box, beaks clamped on a row
of twitching insects for their mouthy chicks.

Birds become intimates and bird-watchers
blind with benevolence: we fail to grasp
the woodpecker's intent as he flies in,
inspects the box, then starts to drill,
scattering savage splinters, while the blue tits
chitter and dive-bomb in a helpless frenzy,
until at last he beaks out a scrawny nestling,

dangles it by one featherless leg
and bears it off to the forest, live and writhing.
Later, as the dark splits like a pumpkin,
spilling orange over the northern sky,
there surfaces from some dark register
of wars the image of a baby bayoneted
at its mother's breast and tossed to the flames.

Äkäsmylly

Mid-morning:
shadows marching north,
the fell gleaming like an egg.

We ski down through the trees,
poles twangling in stiff snow
like a jew's harp.

Nothing of man's making here
but a cluster of wooden huts
hugging frozen ground.

An old man whistles birds
into a snow-white birch:
they drop down flashing cinnamon
to feed from his hand.

He names them in his own tongue,
nodding and smiling: kuukkelit,
Siberian jays.

In his smoke-dark cabin
furnished with reindeer skins
he hangs his mobile on an antler,
brews us bitter coffee.

Mole-blind and dozy, we stumble out
to the old wheel and the grinding stone;
listen to water talking to itself
beneath the ice.

The air is charged with tiny crystals,
each one a glittering prism.
Everything is in perfect poise,
all held in one sacred point of stillness
in the flow of things.

Whatever may be lost
after we ski across the bridge
into the trees, into other lives,
this much is sealed:

an old man reaching out his hand
to the Siberian jays, kuukkelit,
nodding and smiling.

Shadows

In a time of shadows
go north, and more north
where the polar curve pulls

and stretches the sky,
where winter light blurs
and flattens dimension.

Stand in the forest,
a place without shadow
where snow feathers drift

unmindful of gravity
this way and that way;
where even the water

deep in its ice bowl
has swallowed the light;
where crimson blooms

in the hooves of reindeer
hacked off and heaped
by the old mill building.

When your bubble of self
has puffed to nothing,
you'll feel suddenly dizzy,

you'll long for the sun
to lean down on the trees,
to print spearheads of spruce

and fountains of birch
the colour of dusk on
the snow's white blindness;

your own shadow also,
your measure of self on
the earth's blank pages.

Nightriders
Norwegian Snowmobile Touring Club

Hardangervidda midnight:
glittering stars ghosted the smooth brow
of the mountain; pale ice muscled and creaked
beneath our sledge as we rode bucking
and swerving over the lake,
cold to the very bone.

The hut was a planet among pinpricks.
Dead of night: we sank into bunks, dead weight;
but the slow thunder of impending doom
invaded our black oblivion,
Thor's hammer on a hundred anvils
plundered the silence.

Helmeted giants, bulked out
in black leather jackets, boots and gauntlets,
circled the hut astride a fleet of gleaming
metal long-ships, goggles a-glint,
headlamps slashing the night.

Their revels harried me through shifting veils
of sleep and rage: greybeards
and huge boys singing and drinking
in the frozen yard, and a pale-faced girl
who lifted her visor to gulp stars.
I swore I hadn't slept a wink
when I woke to the muffled solace of white,
discovered snow had erased all traces
of the night riders.

Hardangervidda daylight:
out on the fells reindeer scattered like twigs.
Fumbling a snowplough down the rutted track,
skis akimbo, I listened for the chime of ice,
for Norsemen raiders riding on the wind,
clashing in the clefts and gullies of the mountain,
deafening the white skies where morning
rode pillion to a crazy night.

Wilderness Looms

Time to return to Ylläshumina,
and I have left the warm shack with the
wood-burner where bobble hats and scarves
dangled from antlers, smelling of wet dog;
where five men stamped cold from their boots,

clasped steaming polystyrene cups
in huge hands, and nodded a Lappish greeting.
Time to embark upon the homeward journey
chasing my ski-tips back along their tracks,
an easy rolling stride, gliding on silk.

Far above, the trees catch winter sunshine,
brief horizontal splendour, barely nudging
clumps of snow-fleece from their thin perches
to drop thudding onto the forest floor.
The day is short. Light thickens and chills.

Thirty degrees of frost burden my limbs,
wilderness looms. I feel the damp embrace
of sweat and fear, pause to conjure
the rasping rhythm of five men hurrying,
hear only my cold breath coming and going,

wonder what they know that I should know,
ponder my inclination to lie down.
Now in the curdled dusk faint lights waver,
beckon deliverance from an adventure
already tarnished with too much anxiety,

though others might have passed the same way
laughing, not seeing over the edge.
A closet coward, I shall rehearse my tale
adding a few heroic fireside flourishes
later, at the bar, with cloudberry liqueurs.

The Clearances

A black-house huddles
beside the track, stubborn against
time and storm;

thick marram thatch
wind-bitten now, leaking light onto
the blackened hearth.

I know the ghosts here,
I've seen them in the old photographs
in Kildonan museum:

men hanging boulders
from the eaves, airing the wet sliced peat
in little dolmens;

women gathering kelp
for the lazy-beds, filling their baskets
on the bitter shore;

children staring
solemnly from dark doorways, from the past.
They are all recorded:

stone lives eroded
by the casual savagery of weather
and wealthy masters.

My bones are cold
with the bruised beauty of it, the
grief of their leaving;

the burden of those
exiled yet unforgotten things
creeled in their hearts:

summer blustering in
buttercup yellow, the storm-dark
rage of winter;

blue beguiling seas;
purple orchids on the machair;
a lapwing's nest.

Chaos Theory

Squinting in cut-glass light high above
the morning-scented pines and the deep ravine
where a storm in a tantrum had chucked
rocks half the size of houses across my path

I watch a butterfly come flip-flopping over
the wild azaleas to land on my leather boot.
It folds wings as creamy-soft as unsalted
Normandy butter, flecked with palest grey.

'What's a flimsy little thing like you doing
in a place like this?' I ask. 'One wet blast
of mountain wind will blow you to oblivion.'
The butterfly purses his pretty, powdery wings.

'This place is bigger than both of us, my friend.
Why should you think yourself the more immune
to sudden onslaughts, better adapted to
survival in such a hostile environment?

I fear you place too much weight on gravity.'
And he lifts off, sashays over purple gentians
to the speckled camouflage of the boulder field .
That night electric storms bombard the mountains.

I mourn the fate of my flighty philosopher,
his delicately dusted wings crushed against
granite crags, while thousands of miles away
a flutter of warm air gives birth to a hurricane.

Otherwise

This was not of our own making
or mistaking:

a falling coconut
thwacking the sand exactly there,
where your head had been

before you gathered yourself,
brushing an ant from your breast,

and stepped out from the shadow
of cool serrated palms

into that salt-diffused brightness
where surf meets shore.

I scoop the coconut from its crater,
the hard green skull of it,

knowing only that each moment is charged
with another kind of ending.

I watch your footprints fill and empty
in hard wet sand,

and out to sea a frigate bird
scripting its killing enterprise,
cursive on white-hot sky,

while in my hand the coconut weighs
heavier than accident or purpose.

Gethsemane

If thou be willing, remove this cup from me.

They are asleep:
they sprawl on the damp grass
gape-mouthed like innocents.

Shoals of moonlight
leap among the olives
and the blood of poppies lies congealed
beneath their folded cloaks.

Stay awake with me, for I am sorrowful.

They have taken refuge:
still dreaming of hosannahs,
they are found wanting at the bitter hour,

deaf to forewarning
that every passionate attachment
forges in its heart the nails
of its betrayal.

Irreconcilables

We're heading west: flamboyant to the last,
the sun performs its famous vanishing act;
our train curves a shining path through fields
of green felt where cows and horses pose
like farmyard toys, rooks hang motionless
on amber air. We too are suspended,
speeding through a rapt emblazoned stillness:
myself, this man with his two solemn sons
in funeral suits, this woman glossy with youth,
all transfixed by the luminous folded hills,
the flaunting sky. How can we reconcile
this gift with its co-existing evils, dark
in the city wilderness, where rich men hunt
in packs, abandoning the dispossessed
to plead their hunger to a mindless sky?

I feel myself plunging like a tomb-stoner
into dark seas of living consciousness
to apprehend the logic of compassion;
if I were to catch someone's eye I'd see
into their soul, embracing as my own
their fear, their fragile hold on love and hope,
like sighting a rare bird that no one else
has noticed yet – something akin to Basho,
weeping his joyous tears, remembering
the ancients, all infirmities forgotten.
We are together on this earth, and may
be glad of it and kind to one another.

The General

A day spent marking time.
He boils eggs for supper,
cuts her toast into soldiers,
flashes back to the desert
and his men sizzling eggs
on the bonnet of a jeep.

I am trained to kill, he thinks,
trying to still the hand
that flutters like a captive bird.
They are in enemy territory
and he knows the campaign
is pretty advanced.

There are daily skirmishes:
he hates the sodden sheets,
food wide of the target, her
snail's pace across the floor;
she hates to see him fretting,
confined to barracks.

Darkness has crept up on them.
Always a man of action,
he washes her face and hands
with a warm flannel, then
opens the window to let in
the soft evening air.

In the border the tall perennials
are marching towards night.
He longs for the desert sky,
the glittering stars like flames
he could reach out and snuff
between finger and thumb.

Ivy

Ivy lies idle in the next bed.
She was a seamstress once, did alterations
at the cleaners till her hands
went knobbly. She says, 'Bring me
something to sew', but her daughter Brenda
who breeds Siamese cats for cat shows
doesn't trust her with a needle.
Brenda thinks dementia's a dirty word,
says her mother's never been the same
since she tripped on the traffic calming.
Ivy says, 'Ssh, they're listening' and takes off
on her zimmer. Yesterday she got out
through the fire escape and all the way
to the car park: cross as two stitches she was
when they found her. 'You are a one'
they said, tut-tutting half-heartedly.
Ivy said, 'I've got to get back,
I left the kettle on.' Her wits are threadbare.
They'll have to move her soon, she's
blocking a bed, but already she's suffered
too many alterations for her liking.
The social worker's been, now Brenda's
telling all and sundry how she can't have her mother,
she's got the cats to look after.
Ivy leans across and taps her nose.
'I'm not daft' she whispers, 'I've left my money
to the cats' home', and she winks.

Home Visit to the Sea

She is sitting up in bed
awash with pain she cannot drown.
'You're late, tide's out,' she rasps
like suck-back over shingle.

She has forgotten me entirely,
her mind adrift, her wits like flotsam
lost on the current, nudging alien reefs,
her storms of grief pounding
an ancient shore.

I feed her fish paste sandwiches,
washed down with salty water (sparkling kind)
while she rocks fretfully, flicking crusts
to the dogfish.

She struggles with winds
and waves of nausea, moon moods,
doldrums, sores;
she dreams tsunamis, sunspots,
icecaps, wrecks.

When we kiss goodbye
she smells of the tide coming in
lively over warm rocks, early evening,
seagulls homing to the islands,
every wet salt surface of the shoreline
swimming red-gold;

then she dismisses me
with one theatrical wave, remembering
just in time to strike a green flash
from the drowning sun.
She will not go quietly.

The Undertaker's Lament

We haven't got a body in the shop*
And no one cares to know the reason why
In August all the dying seems to stop

The undertaker's business tends to flop
With summer's late arrival in July
We haven't got a body in the shop

From January to March a steady crop
Of ancients forms our main supply
In August all the dying seems to stop

Our turnover in May and June's a sop
But come the silly season death grows shy
We haven't got a body in the shop

In Autumn like the hedgerow fruits they drop
Acknowledging a decent time to die
In August all the dying seems to stop

The body count at Christmas reaches top
Our profit loss in August we decry
We haven't got a body in the shop

The crematorium furnace is de trop
Respectful suits and coffins idle lie
We haven't got a body in the shop
In August all the dying seems to stop

*Overheard in the undertaker's office.

Shimla

To my father, born 1911, Central Provinces, India

I crossed a hundred years
and many thousand miles to reach
your natal landscape,
never having asked the questions
that now haunt me.

On your journey from the stifling plains,
was there a woman in a scarlet sari,
working the fields of stubbled gold?
And did the bronze sun float at smoky dusk
above a million fires?

Perhaps your ayah sang you gentler songs
as you began to climb the ribs of hills
towards this summer sanctuary
where pine trees cast their needle nets
to catch the cooling air.

And when they took you
to the English home you'd never known
and left you there, how often in the dulled
and unrelenting winters did you hunger
for the soft rustling of your mother's silks,
the plush of tiger fur beneath
your little feet?

Those were the years of your partition,
born of necessity and grief.
When you next met, you called your father 'Sir',
your mother 'Laddhu'*: they too paid the price
for doing, as we all do in our time,
what they believed was right.

In this forgiving land where you were born
into the ceaseless press of human lives,
the tribulations of another age,
I close the circle as a craftsman sets
the final precious stone of his pietra dura,
knowing we are both at peace.

* *sweetmeat*

Another Day

This day in Amritsar, vertiginous
with vibrant piety and gilded glamour
at the Golden Temple, we take refuge
in Jallianwala Bagh, the massacre
remembrance garden.

Here less than a hundred years ago
a British brigadier ordered his troops
to open fire on a peaceful gathering:
here are the bullet holes in the stone walls,
traces of blood like faded canna lilies;
here is the well into which they leapt
to a bloody drowning. Sixteen hundred and
fifty rounds, and almost as many Indians
piled on a human rag-heap.

Today in Jallianwala Bagh
a clutch of pilgrims wanders peaceably
beneath the trees, their only respite
from the bludgeoning white light; children race
from the martyrs' well to the memorial,
where shadows of a bad conscience darken:
here we wear the skin of the oppressor,
we are branded with his savagery.

When the young man touches me I flinch,
but he just wants a shot of me with his wife
and children: I am a harmless spectacle
in my English memsahib hat; so we shuffle up,
link arms and smile and smile at the camera,
un-remembering.

Perhaps they'll make their own connections later,
setting this photograph alongside others
from the faded archive of atrocities.
Brigadier Dyer was convinced he'd done
a jolly good thing, but I am mortified,
this day in Amritsar.

There Be Dragons

They knew a thing or two, the old map-makers:
there beyond the edge of west half visible
among the tangled mists they hatched their dragons.
These are not quaint domesticated creatures,
but emblems of outer darkness and unknowing.

Covetous men squaring their sails to plunder
rode the dark seas as they rode strong horses,
making believe for a time they were the masters.
There was no certainty that any vessel
would not fall off the known rim of the world.

Still there be dragons, though we banished them
from the arrogant cartography of reason:
like the ancient wyrm that rises from the darkness
they haunt the margins, exiled but not extinguished,
mapped in the terra incognita of the mind.

Shadow Selves

They are there in the dark of us,
shackled and dungeoned
out of mind.

We pass them cups of water,
scraps of bread,
curious to look into their eyes
and see our own violence
shining there.

Sometimes when we need the spice
of power or pain
we let them out;

mostly we shut them up
like the Inuit woman
who went about all winter

gathering shadows into boxes
so that when spring came
there would be light.

The Rope Bridge

So slender, so frayed, the rope bridge
slung across the chasm -
easy to put a foot through the rotting slats,
anyone could fall.

A tiny lapse of concentration and
you lose your balance.
There's no resisting the pull of gravity,
it becomes too much

to keep going, keep talking, keep needing,
keep wanting to survive,
and one day you just can't be bothered
to get out of bed,

get dressed, go to work, read the mail,
pay the bills, so your
skin silts with grime, teeth rot, armpits sour;
you no longer notice

dark stains in the basin, blood stains
on the blankets,
and one day you wake under an archway
in a cardboard box.

Nobody cares if you jumped or if you were
so to speak pushed;
the roar of the river drowns your cries,
only your mother keeps vigil

cradling a sliver of hope, while those of us
with a head for heights
(don't look down, there but for the grace etc.)
take another step.

Bequest

Let me tell you how it is:
the world is darkening.

I never thought to warn my children
to be childless:
I would rather point them to the orchard,
tell them to lie under the cherry blossom,
guarding the spirit while the flesh
makes flesh.

But there is too much of everything
or too little.
The elements are confused:
fire smoulders with ancient grudges,
poisoning the air; earth and water wander
dispossessed.
We have learned nothing or forgotten
what we knew.

At the check-in desk a young man
with elsewhere eyes hugs his violin case
and we are afraid.
This is what we have done to ourselves,
blind followers of the blind,
tapping our long white wands towards
the precipice.

You will tell me it was always so,
for every age fresh lamentations.
My children in their turn
will go to the orchard for the sweet green shade,
for stripping the fruit,
for planting saplings I shall not live to see
grow tall and beautiful.

Larks
Talis, inquiens, mihi videtur, rex, vita hominum praesens in terris*

The planes fly low,
roll over, languidly tipping their wings,
practising death.

Our present certainty
lies in a harrier's flight through the bright hall
of a Dartmoor sky

yet in the slipstream
of silence larks fling theme and variation
from blue to blue,

seen and not seen
like shifting specks on the surface of the eye.
War is elsewhere:

some trickery of conscience
cleanses us like wind-picked bones among
the bleached grasses

and all the lively
afternoon larks dance to a music we never
thought to hear again.

* 'Such,' he said, 'O King, seems to me the present life of men on earth ....
as if a single sparrow should fly swiftly into the hall, and coming in at one
door, instantly fly out through another.'
from Bede's Historia Ecclesiastica.

Thin Ice

Once in your figurative innocence
you signified nothing more sinister
than straying from the safety of the shore;
we were not schooled in your fragility
and breaking point, how ice like intimacy
forms and weakens at the edges first.

You kept your secrets well: the hapless carp
trapped gape-mouthed in glazed suburban ponds;
Franklin's sailors coffined in permafrost
their bones still harbouring the taint of lead;
Otzi ice-mummified with bow and boots
and a belly full of undigested grain.

Now time moves swiftly to unmantle truth:
not long ago we fretted for the ferns
that frosted childhood panes, or clownish ducks
crash-landing in the park; but now we mourn
your glaciers slinking to their ancient lairs,
your ice-sheets dwindling under poisoned skies.

For you are the emblem of catastrophe,
and we like arctic villagers who fix
a marker in the freezing Ounasjoki,
betting on the day when spring the saboteur
will loosen your clenched fist and fling the post
with all its freight of hopes into oblivion.

Sorry

Sorry for the burnt saucepan
The shrunken T-shirt
The broken cup

Sorry for the unkind word
The selfish deed
The bad mood

Sorry for the bent fender
The road rage
The pile-ups

Sorry for the battery chicks
The gassed badger
The hunted fox

Sorry for the homeless youth
The beaten wife
The raped child

Sorry for the displaced peoples
The shipped slaves
The vanished tribes

Sorry for the genocide
The disappeared
The tortured

Sorry for the holocaust

Sorry for the starving millions
The half-truths
The bribes

Sorry for the careless bullet
The car-bomb
The corpses

Sorry for the hurricane
The earth-quake
The tsunami

Sorry for the melting ice
The ozone layer
The felled forests

Sorry for not caring enough
Not saying enough
Not doing enough

Sorry for the heedlessness
The godlessness
The greed

Sorry

Human Writes ...

Purely on the off-chance you may be out there
(if I may use the personal form of address)
I'm writing to let you know things don't look good.
I'm not surprised you've given us up as a bad job,
but it's one thing to be the kind of boss who likes
to set everything up and then leaves his brainchild
to work out its own salvation, quite another to pull
the plug so your baby goes out with the bathwater.

(I've just been out to check up on things. The river's
running low and all the animals are restless).

I honestly don't know why we end up hurting
one another. There may have been something faulty
in your design: free will, for example, is definitely
a double-edged gift. Mess up, and it's nobody's fault
but our own. But hey, even the most post-modernist
god-head must want to see his or her
creation reach its targets. Give us a break.

(A bird has just thrown itself at the window and fallen.
At a time like this everything seems like an omen).

I can understand you being angry with us for poaching
your secrets, encroaching on your almightiness,
for screwing up our stewardship of the earth,
and discounting the voices of all the trouble-shooters
you've sent us over the years, but can't you see
that what's happening down here is disproportionate?
We've always done things our way, it's hard to change.

I haven't told anyone about getting in touch with you:
they'd think I was mad or dangerous, or plotting
a hostile takeover, but I believe in hedging my bets.
It may seem a bit presumptuous, but I also believe
I am worth promoting. Am I too aspirational?

(A small child brings me the body of the dead bird,
still warm, and asks why the sky is a funny colour).

If there's anyone out there, for heaven's sake
are you just going to let it end like this, washing
your hands of us, to be or not to be, whatever?
Heaven helps those who help themselves, right,
but surely the buck stops with the one at the top.

(The sunsets, I've noticed, are getting redder and redder).

Other books published by Oversteps

Anthologies: Company of Poets and Company of Four
David Grubb: An Alphabet of Light
Giles Goodland: Littoral
Alex Smith: Keyserling
Will Daunt: Running out of England
Patricia Bishop: Saving Dragons & Time's Doppelgänger
Christopher Cook: For and Against Nature
Jan Farquarson: No dammed tears
Charles Hadfield: The nothing we sink or swim in
Mandy Pannett: Bee Purple & Frost Hollow
Doris Hulme: Planted with stones
James Cole: From the Blue
Helen Kitson: Tesserae
Bill Headdon: Picardy.com
Avril Bruten: In the lost & found columns
Ross Cogan: Stalin's desk
Ann Kelley: Because we have reached that place
Marianne Larsen: A Common Language
Anne Lewis-Smith: Every seventh wave
Mary Maher: green darlings
Susan Taylor: The suspension of the moon
Simon Williams: Quirks
Genista Lewes: Cat's Cradle
Alwyn Marriage: Touching Earth
Miriam Darlington: Windfall
Anne Born & Glen Phillips: Singing Granites
A C Clarke: Messages of Change
Rebecca Gethin: River is the Plural of Rain
W H Petty: But someone liked them
Melanie Penycate: Feeding Humming Birds
Andrew Nightingale: The Big Wheel
Caroline Carver: Three Hares
John Stuart: Word of Mouth
Ann Segrave: Aviatrix
Rose Cook: Taking Flight
Jenny Hope: Petrolhead
Christopher North: Explaining the Circumstances
Hilary Elfick: An Ordinary Storm
Jennie Osborne: How to be Naked

www.overstepsbooks.com